THE WRAP COOKBOOK

The Complete Guide to Simple Techniques & Creative Combinations for Fresh, Flavorful Meals

LEIGH D. WHEELER

Copyright © 2024 By LEIGH D. WHEELER. All rights reserved worldwide.

No part of this book may be reproduced or transmitted in any form or by any means, electronic or mechanical, including photocopying, recording, or by any information storage and retrieval system, without written permission from the publisher, except for the inclusion of brief quotations in a review.

Warning-Disclaimer:

The purpose of this book is to educate and entertain. The author or publisher does not guarantee that anyone following the techniques, suggestions, tips, ideas, or strategies will become successful. The author and publisher shall have neither liability nor responsibility to anyone with respect to any loss or damage caused, or alleged to be caused, directly or indirectly, by the information contained in this book.

This copyright notice and disclaimer apply to the entirety of the book and its contents, whether in print or electronic form, and extend to all future editions or revisions of the book. Unauthorized use or reproduction of this book or its contents is strictly prohibited and may result in legal action.

Table of Contents

INTRODUCTION 6
   DEFINITION OF WRAPS 6

CULTURAL SIGNIFICANCE AND VARIATIONS OF WRAPS 9

BENEFITS OF WRAPS 12

WRAP ESSENTIALS 16

Chapter 1: Breakfast Wraps 20
   1. Spinach and Feta Egg Wrap 20
   2. Avocado and Bacon Breakfast Wrap 20
   3. Berry Yogurt and Granola Wrap 21
   4. Scrambled Tofu and Veggie Wrap 21
   5. Peanut Butter Banana Wrap 22
   6. Smoked Salmon and Cream Cheese Wrap 22
   7. Veggie Omelette Wrap 23
   8. Breakfast Burrito Wrap 23
   9. Chia Seed Pudding Wrap 24
   10. Sweet Potato and Black Bean Wrap 24

Chapter 2: Lunch Wraps 25
   1. Turkey and Hummus Wrap 25
   2. Mediterranean Veggie Wrap 25
   3. Chicken Caesar Salad Wrap 26
   4. BBQ Pulled Pork Wrap 26
   5. Caprese Wrap with Pesto 27
   6. Quinoa and Roasted Veggie Wrap 27
   7. Tuna Salad Wrap 28
   8. Greek Chicken Wrap 28
   9. Falafel and Tzatziki Wrap 29
   10. Cucumber and Cream Cheese Wrap 29

Chapter 3: Dinner Wraps 30
   1. Teriyaki Chicken Wrap 30
   2. Beef and Broccoli Wrap 30

3. Shrimp Taco Wrap 31

4. Vegetarian Stir-Fry Wrap 31

5. Chicken Fajita Wrap 32

6. Pesto Pasta and Chicken Wrap 32

7. Moroccan Spiced Lamb Wrap 33

8. Stuffed Bell Pepper Wrap 33

9. Coconut Curry Chicken Wrap 34

10. Moussaka Wrap 34

Chapter 4: Snack Wraps 35

1. Cheese and Apple Wrap 35

2. Veggie Sticks and Hummus Wrap 35

3. Nut Butter and Fruit Wrap 36

4. Popcorn and Cheddar Wrap 36

5. Antipasto Skewers Wrap 37

6. Sweet and Savory Trail Mix Wrap 37

7. Energy Bar Wrap 38

8. Salsa and Guacamole Wrap 38

9. Chocolate Banana Wrap 39

10. Crispy Chickpea Wrap 39

Chapter 5: Vegetarian Wraps 40

1. Roasted Vegetable Wrap 40

2. Spicy Black Bean Wrap 40

3. Lentil Salad Wrap 41

4. Grilled Eggplant and Zucchini Wrap 41

5. Chickpea Salad Wrap 42

6. Caprese Pesto Wrap 42

7. Stuffed Portobello Mushroom Wrap 43

8. Ratatouille Wrap 43

9. Curried Cauliflower Wrap 44

10. Spinach and Ricotta Wrap 44

Chapter 6: Vegan Wraps 45

1. Tofu and Vegetable Stir-Fry Wrap 45

2. Roasted Beet and Avocado Wrap 45

3. Chickpea and Avocado Mash Wrap 46

4. Vegan BBQ Jackfruit Wrap 46

5. Sweet Potato and Kale Wrap 47

6. Thai Peanut Tofu Wrap 47

7. Zucchini Noodle Wrap 48

8. Mango and Black Bean Wrap 48

9. Cabbage and Rice Wrap 49

10. Lemon-Dill Quinoa Wrap 49

Chapter 7: Gluten-Free Wraps 50

1. Cauliflower Wrap with Grilled Chicken 50

2. Rice Paper Veggie Wrap 50

3. Lettuce Wrap with Ground Turkey 51

4. Chickpea Flour Wrap with Spinach 51

5. Polenta and Roasted Vegetable Wrap 51

6. Quinoa and Avocado Wrap 52

7. Sweet Potato and Black Bean Lettuce Wrap 52

8. Eggplant Parmesan Wrap 53

9. Grilled Fish and Mango Wrap 53

10. Savory Oat Wrap 54

Chapter 8: International Wraps 55

1. Greek Souvlaki Wrap 55

2. Vietnamese Banh Mi Wrap 55

3. Mexican Burrito Wrap 56

4. Indian Paneer Tikka Wrap 56

5. Japanese Sushi Wrap 57

6. Korean BBQ Beef Wrap 57

7. Italian Panini Wrap 58

8. Thai Spring Roll Wrap 58

9. Lebanese Shawarma Wrap 59

10. Cuban Sandwich Wrap 59

Chapter 9: Kids' Wraps 60

1. Peanut Butter and Jelly Wrap 60
2. Turkey and Cheese Roll-Up Wrap 60
3. Fruit and Yogurt Wrap 61
4. Ham and Cheese Pretzel Wrap 61
5. Mini Pizza Wrap 61
6. Nutella and Banana Wrap 62
7. Chicken Nuggets Wrap 62
8. Rainbow Veggie Wrap 63
9. Mac and Cheese Wrap 63
10. Marshmallow and Chocolate Wrap 63

Chapter 10: Creative Wraps 65

1. Sushi-Style Wrap with Quinoa 65
2. Dessert Waffle Wrap 65
3. Pizza-Flavored Wrap 66
4. Nacho Wrap with Cheese and Salsa 66
5. S'mores Wrap 67
6. Macaroni and Cheese Wrap 67
7. Caesar Salad Pizza Wrap 68
8. Breakfast Smoothie Wrap 68
9. Spinach and Artichoke Dip Wrap 69
10. Chocolate Hazelnut Spread Wrap 69

CONCLUSION 70

INTRODUCTION

DEFINITION OF WRAPS

Wraps are a versatile and convenient way to enjoy a variety of foods, all neatly bundled into a portable format. Essentially, a wrap is any type of filling—be it meats, vegetables, or spreads—enclosed in a flatbread or similar base. The beauty of wraps lies in their adaptability; they can be a hearty meal, a light snack, or even a sweet treat, depending on what you choose to include.

In its simplest form, a wrap is created by placing ingredients on a flat surface, rolling it up, and then enjoying it on the go. Whether you're using a tortilla, lettuce leaf, rice paper, or nori, the possibilities are endless. You can experiment with textures, flavours, and cuisines, making wraps an excellent choice for both everyday meals and special occasions.

History of Wraps

The history of wraps is as diverse as the cultures that create them. Though wraps in their various forms can be traced back centuries, their popularity has surged in modern times. Let's take a closer look at some historical contexts that shaped what we now consider wraps.

Ancient Origins

The concept of wrapping food can be traced back to ancient civilizations. Flatbreads, which form the base for many wraps today, have been around for thousands of years. In the Middle East, for instance, the use of pita bread to encase meats and vegetables has been a tradition for millennia. This method not only preserves the food but also makes it easier to eat, especially in communal settings.

In China, the tradition of wrapping food also has deep roots. The popular spring roll features a thin dough filled with various ingredients, which is then rolled and often fried. This technique emphasizes the idea that wrapping can enhance the flavours and presentation of food.

Cultural Variations

As we moved through history, different cultures adapted the idea of wraps to their unique ingredients and culinary traditions. In Mexico, the tortilla evolved as a staple food, giving rise to burritos and tacos, both of which are forms of wraps. The combination of beans, meats, and spices wrapped in a tortilla became a cultural icon, celebrated for its robust flavours and portability.

In Japan, sushi rolls are another perfect example of wraps. Nori, a seaweed sheet, is used to encase seasoned rice along with various fillings, creating a compact and delightful meal that has gained international acclaim. Similarly, the Vietnamese bánh mì features a baguette—another form of a wrap—filled with meats, pickled vegetables, and fresh herbs, showcasing a fusion of French and Vietnamese culinary traditions.

Modern Popularity

In recent decades, wraps have become a staple in cafés and fast-casual restaurants worldwide. With the rise of health-conscious eating, wraps have been marketed as a healthier alternative to traditional sandwiches, often filled with fresh vegetables, lean proteins, and whole grains. Their versatility means they can be tailored to fit various diets, from vegetarian to gluten-free options.

I remember my first encounter with a wrap during a casual lunch out with friends. I opted for a classic chicken Caesar wrap, and it was love at first bite. The crisp lettuce, juicy chicken, and creamy dressing rolled into a soft tortilla was an experience that opened my eyes to the world of wraps. It was a meal that felt indulgent yet wholesome, making it a go-to option for busy days.

Health and Lifestyle

Wraps have earned a place in many households, especially among families seeking quick, nutritious meals. With their ability to incorporate a variety of food groups, wraps allow for balanced eating while still being fun and interactive. I've found that getting my kids involved in the wrapping process not only makes meals more enjoyable but also encourages them to try new ingredients.

The wrap craze has also led to the emergence of innovative products like cauliflower tortillas and whole grain wraps, catering to dietary preferences and restrictions. Whether you're gluten-free, vegan, or simply looking to reduce carbs, there's likely a wrap option that suits your needs.

The Wrap Experience

Creating wraps can be a delightful experience. The process is not only about assembling ingredients; it's also about experimenting with flavours and textures. I often find myself rummaging through the fridge, looking for leftovers to use as filling. The thrill of discovering a new combination—like roasted vegetables with a dollop of hummus or leftover grilled chicken with fresh herbs—makes cooking feel less like a chore and more like a creative adventure.

I encourage you to think outside the box when it comes to wraps. You can mix and match cuisines, combining elements from different cultures to create something uniquely yours. A Mediterranean-inspired wrap with falafel, tabbouleh, and tahini can easily sit next to an Asian-style wrap filled with teriyaki chicken and crunchy veggies.

As we embark on this journey through the world of wraps, I hope you feel inspired to explore and experiment. The principles of wraps are grounded in simplicity and creativity. They allow us to enjoy delicious meals without the fuss. With just a few basic ingredients and a willingness to try new combinations, anyone can master the art of wrapping.

Whether you're preparing a quick lunch for yourself or crafting a family-friendly dinner, wraps offer an easy, satisfying solution. So, roll up your sleeves, gather your ingredients, and let's dive into the wonderful world of wraps together!

CULTURAL SIGNIFICANCE AND VARIATIONS OF WRAPS

The Global Tapestry of Wraps

Wraps are more than just a practical way to eat; they embody the culinary heritage and cultural nuances of the regions from which they originate. Each variation tells a story, reflecting local ingredients, cooking techniques, and historical influences. As we explore the cultural significance of wraps, I invite you to consider how these simple bundles connect us to traditions and communities around the world.

Middle Eastern Roots

One of the oldest and most beloved forms of wraps can be found in Middle Eastern cuisine. The pita, a round flatbread, serves as a perfect pocket for a myriad of fillings. From shawarma to falafel, these wraps highlight the vibrant flavours of the region, combining spices, fresh vegetables, and protein in a convenient format.

Growing up, I often enjoyed homemade falafel wraps filled with crisp lettuce, tomatoes, and a drizzle of tahini. These wraps weren't just meals; they were a way to connect with my heritage. Sharing a plate of falafel wraps with family during special occasions became a cherished tradition, reinforcing the idea that food is a powerful means of bringing people together.

Mexican Influence

In Mexico, the tortilla is a fundamental staple, offering a foundation for a multitude of wraps, such as burritos and tacos. Each region in Mexico has its own unique take on wraps, influenced by local ingredients and culinary practices. For instance, in the Yucatán, you might find cochinita pibil—a slow-cooked, spiced pork—wrapped in soft corn tortillas.

I remember the first time I tasted a burrito filled with smoky chipotle chicken and black beans. It was a revelation! The warm tortilla cradled a hearty filling, making each bite a delicious adventure. Mexican wraps not only showcase rich flavours but also reflect the country's cultural diversity, highlighting how food can convey identity and history.

Asian Innovations

In Asia, wraps take on various forms and styles, often incorporating rice or vegetables as the base. Take the Vietnamese bánh mì, for example. This delightful sandwich combines a crispy baguette with pickled vegetables, fresh herbs, and marinated meats, embodying the fusion of French and Vietnamese culinary influences.

Sushi rolls from Japan also exemplify the art of wrapping. Nori, a type of seaweed, encases vinegared rice and an array of fillings, from fresh fish to vegetables. Sushi rolls have become globally popular, not just for their taste but also for their aesthetic appeal.

I recall a summer picnic where I packed homemade sushi rolls for my friends. The vibrant colours of the ingredients made them look like little works of art, and watching everyone's eyes light up when they took a bite was a joy. It reminded me that wraps are not only about convenience—they can also be a canvas for creativity.

Mediterranean Flair

The Mediterranean region offers its own variety of wraps, often featuring fresh ingredients and robust flavours. The Greek souvlaki wrap is a delightful example, filled with grilled meats, fresh vegetables, and tangy tzatziki sauce. This wrap is a testament to the Mediterranean's emphasis on using fresh, seasonal produce.

During a trip to Greece, I enjoyed souvlaki wraps at a bustling street market. The aroma of grilled meats wafted through the air, enticing passersby to stop for a quick bite. The combination of warm pita, juicy chicken, and refreshing tzatziki was unforgettable. It's moments like these that illustrate how wraps serve as a delicious and convenient way to experience a culture.

The Evolution in Western Cuisine

In recent years, wraps have gained popularity in Western countries as a quick, healthy alternative to traditional sandwiches. Fast-casual dining establishments have embraced wraps, offering a range of fillings that cater to health-conscious consumers. From protein-packed options to gluten-free and vegan varieties, wraps have adapted to meet the diverse needs of modern diners.

I often find myself gravitating toward wraps when I want something quick yet satisfying. A wrap filled with grilled chicken, mixed greens, and a light dressing becomes my go-to lunch when I'm on the move. The versatility of wraps allows for endless combinations, ensuring there's something for everyone.

Cultural Significance

Wraps hold cultural significance far beyond their convenience. They represent the culinary traditions of various societies, each with its own unique story to tell. In many cultures, food is a central part of social gatherings, and wraps often play a starring role.

For instance, during family celebrations, it's common to see platters of wraps being shared among guests. The act of gathering around food fosters connections and creates lasting memories. I cherish the moments spent with loved ones, crafting wraps together and sharing our favourite fillings. These experiences reinforce the idea that food can bridge gaps and bring people closer.

Personal Experience with Wraps

As I reflect on my own journey with wraps, I realise how much they have enriched my culinary experiences. I've had the pleasure of trying wraps from various cultures, each one teaching me something new about the world.

For example, during a trip to Morocco, I tasted a delicious Moroccan wrap filled with spiced lamb and roasted vegetables, all wrapped in soft flatbread. The combination of spices transported me to another place, illustrating how food can be an adventure in itself.

In my kitchen, I've experimented with different styles of wraps, often inviting friends and family to join me. Hosting a wrap-making night has become a fun tradition, where everyone brings their favourite ingredients. We share stories, laughter, and, of course, delicious food. These moments are a testament to the joy that wraps can bring to our lives.

Wraps are more than just a way to hold ingredients together; they are a reflection of cultural heritage, creativity, and community. As we explore the world of wraps throughout this cookbook, I hope you feel inspired to appreciate the rich tapestry of flavours and traditions they represent. Embrace the opportunity to experiment and create your own wrap variations, and remember that each wrap you make carries a bit of the world's culinary history with it.

BENEFITS OF WRAPS

Wraps are not just delicious; they also come with a host of benefits that make them a fantastic option for anyone looking to improve their eating habits. Whether you're a busy professional, a parent on the go, or just someone wanting to enjoy wholesome food, wraps can fit seamlessly into your lifestyle. In this section, we'll explore the nutritional advantages, versatility, and convenience of wraps, offering insights from my personal experiences along the way.

Nutritional Advantages

A Balanced Meal in One Package

One of the most compelling reasons to incorporate wraps into your diet is their ability to offer balanced nutrition in a single, easy-to-eat package. When you think about a wrap, you can easily fill it with a variety of food groups: proteins, carbohydrates, vegetables, and healthy fats. This balance can make it simpler to meet your nutritional needs without needing to prepare multiple dishes.

For example, I often whip up a wrap filled with grilled chicken, avocado, mixed greens, and a dollop of hummus. This combination not only provides protein from the chicken but also healthy fats from the avocado and a good dose of fibre and vitamins from the greens. It's a complete meal that leaves me feeling satisfied without being overly full.

Fresh Ingredients, Fresh Benefits

Wraps encourage the use of fresh ingredients. Most wraps can be made using vegetables, lean proteins, and whole grains, which are all key components of a healthy diet. Leafy greens, tomatoes, cucumbers, peppers, and a variety of herbs add vital nutrients and antioxidants, helping to boost overall health.

I remember experimenting with a Mediterranean wrap packed with spinach, roasted red peppers, and feta cheese. The vibrant colours were not just appealing to the eye; they also indicated a wealth of nutrients. Fresh vegetables are essential for maintaining energy levels and supporting overall well-being.

Portion Control Made Easy

Wraps can also assist with portion control. Unlike traditional sandwiches, where it can be easy to pile on too much filling or add unnecessary condiments, wraps often allow for more manageable portions. This can be particularly beneficial if you're trying to watch your calorie intake or simply want to avoid overeating.

When making wraps for my family, I've found that each person can easily customise their own wrap to fit their appetite. If someone wants a lighter option, they can use fewer ingredients, while others can load up their wraps with extra fillings. This flexibility makes it easier for everyone to enjoy a meal that suits their needs.

Alternative Ingredients for Dietary Needs

The world of wraps is also incredibly accommodating for various dietary needs. Whether you're gluten-free, vegan, or following a low-carb diet, you can easily adapt wraps to fit your lifestyle. Many shops now offer alternative wraps made from ingredients like cauliflower, chickpeas, or even lettuce leaves, which allow for creativity without sacrificing nutritional value.

For instance, I've enjoyed using large lettuce leaves as a substitute for traditional wraps. They provide a satisfying crunch and allow me to enjoy all the fillings without the added carbohydrates. These adaptations make wraps a versatile option for anyone looking to maintain a healthy lifestyle.

Versatility and Convenience

Endless Combinations

One of the most exciting aspects of wraps is their endless versatility. You can fill them with almost anything you desire—meats, vegetables, spreads, and even fruits. This flexibility means you can easily tailor wraps to fit different tastes, occasions, and cuisines.

For instance, I love experimenting with international flavours. One night, I might prepare a spicy Mexican wrap with beans, avocado, and salsa. The next, I could switch gears and create a Thai-inspired wrap using marinated tofu, shredded carrots, and a peanut sauce. This ability to switch it up keeps me engaged in the kitchen and prevents me from falling into a monotonous routine.

Quick and Easy Preparation

In today's fast-paced world, time is often of the essence. Wraps are a fantastic solution when you're short on time but still want to enjoy a wholesome meal. The preparation is quick and straightforward—most wraps can be assembled in under 15 minutes.

When I find myself in a rush, I often turn to my trusty wraps. I keep a selection of pre-washed salad greens, sliced veggies, and cooked proteins in the fridge, ready to go. A simple assembly of these ingredients in a wrap can create a nutritious meal in no time. I've even made wraps in the car while on road trips!

Meal Prep and Planning Made Simple

Wraps are excellent for meal prep. You can prepare fillings in advance, store them in the fridge, and assemble your wraps as needed throughout the week. This makes it easier to stick to healthy eating habits when life gets busy.

During weekends, I like to batch cook proteins like grilled chicken or roasted vegetables, then store them in separate containers. On a Monday, I can grab my ingredients, roll them up, and have a delicious lunch ready to take to work. This kind of meal planning not only saves time but also ensures I'm eating nourishing food throughout the week.

Kid-Friendly Fun

Wraps can be an enjoyable option for kids, as they allow for a hands-on approach to meals. Children can get involved in the assembly process, choosing their favourite ingredients and making their own creations. This not only makes mealtime more exciting but also encourages children to try new foods.

I often host "wrap parties" with my kids, where we lay out various ingredients and let them assemble their wraps. Watching their creativity unfold as they combine flavours they love is always a joy. Plus, it helps teach them valuable skills about food preparation and making healthier choices.

Perfect for Any Occasion

Wraps are incredibly versatile when it comes to occasions. Whether you're hosting a casual lunch with friends, preparing a picnic, or even serving food at a party, wraps can be easily adapted to fit any scenario.

For a recent gathering, I prepared a variety of wraps, including a classic chicken Caesar, a vegetarian Mediterranean option, and even a dessert wrap filled with Nutella and strawberries. Each guest could choose what appealed to them, making it a fun and interactive meal that catered to diverse tastes.

Health on the Go

In a world where convenience often comes at the expense of nutrition, wraps provide a solution that doesn't compromise health for speed. They are easy to transport, making them an ideal choice for lunchboxes, picnics, or on-the-go meals.

I've found that packing a wrap for lunch keeps me satisfied throughout the day. It's easy to eat at my desk or take to a picnic without worrying about spills or mess. With a wrap in hand, I can enjoy a nutritious meal no matter where I am.

The benefits of wraps extend far beyond mere convenience; they offer a wealth of nutritional advantages, versatility, and ease that can enhance any diet. By integrating wraps into your meals, you can enjoy balanced nutrition, embrace creativity in the kitchen, and simplify your meal preparation.

As you explore the recipes in this cookbook, I encourage you to think about the various ways wraps can fit into your life. Experiment with different fillings, involve your family in the preparation process, and relish the joy of creating meals that not only nourish your body but also bring a sense of fun and excitement to the table. Whether you're making a quick lunch or planning a gathering, wraps are sure to impress and satisfy.

WRAP ESSENTIALS

Wraps are incredibly versatile, allowing you to mix and match a variety of ingredients to create meals that suit your tastes and dietary preferences. To make the most of your wrap experience, it's important to understand the different types of wraps and the key ingredients that go into them. In this section, we'll explore the various wrap options available and highlight essential components for crafting the perfect wrap.

Types of Wraps

Tortillas

Tortillas are perhaps the most common type of wrap, particularly in Mexican and Tex-Mex cuisines. Made from flour or corn, they provide a soft, pliable base that can easily hold a wide range of fillings.

Flour Tortillas: These are often larger and softer than their corn counterparts, making them ideal for burritos and wraps that require more substantial fillings. I love using flour tortillas for my chicken fajita wraps, as they fold beautifully around the grilled chicken and veggies.

Corn Tortillas: These are typically smaller and have a distinct, slightly sweet flavour. They're perfect for tacos or smaller wraps. I enjoy using corn tortillas for making breakfast tacos filled with scrambled eggs and salsa—they're both satisfying and quick to prepare.

Lettuce Leaves

For a lighter, low-carb option, lettuce leaves are fantastic wraps. Varieties like iceberg, romaine, or butter lettuce provide a crisp texture and a refreshing crunch.

I often turn to lettuce wraps when I want something that feels fresh and healthy. A personal favourite is a chicken lettuce wrap filled with seasoned chicken, grated carrots, and a drizzle of soy sauce. The crunch of the lettuce adds a delightful contrast to the tender chicken.

Nori

Nori is a type of seaweed that's commonly used in Japanese cuisine, especially for sushi. Nori wraps are typically filled with sushi rice, fish, vegetables, and various sauces.

My first experience with nori wraps was when I tried making sushi at home. It was a fun and creative process! I remember filling the nori with sticky rice, avocado, and fresh salmon, then rolling it up tight. The combination of flavours was incredible, and I felt proud to create something so delicious.

Rice Paper

Rice paper is another option that's often used in Vietnamese spring rolls. It's thin, translucent, and pliable when soaked in water, making it ideal for wrapping a variety of fillings.

I love making fresh spring rolls with rice paper. The process is quite simple: just dip the rice paper in warm water until it's soft, then layer in ingredients like shrimp, vermicelli noodles, and fresh herbs. These wraps are not only delicious but also visually stunning, making them perfect for gatherings.

Pita Bread

Pita bread is a Middle Eastern staple that can be used as a wrap by cutting it in half and stuffing it with fillings. It's thick and chewy, providing a sturdy base for meats, veggies, and sauces.

One of my favourite meals is a homemade falafel pita wrap. I fill the pita with crispy falafel, creamy tahini sauce, and a medley of fresh vegetables. The combination of textures and flavours never fails to satisfy!

Other Alternatives

In addition to these popular types of wraps, there are many other options available. Some people enjoy using whole grain or gluten-free wraps, which come in various flavours and textures. You might also encounter wraps made from unique ingredients like chickpea flour or even sweet potato.

I've tried experimenting with different types of wraps to find what suits my taste best. Each offers its own unique flavour and texture, allowing for endless creativity in the kitchen.

Key Ingredients for Wraps

To create a delicious and satisfying wrap, it's essential to have a variety of key ingredients on hand. The best wraps typically contain a balance of proteins, vegetables, and sauces. Let's dive into each of these components.

Proteins

Proteins are crucial for making your wraps filling and nutritious. Depending on your dietary preferences, you can choose from a variety of sources:

Meats: Chicken, beef, pork, and turkey are popular choices for hearty wraps. I often grill chicken breasts and slice them for use in various wraps. A classic chicken Caesar wrap is a staple in my house, combining grilled chicken with romaine lettuce, parmesan cheese, and creamy dressing.

Fish and Seafood: Fish such as salmon or tuna can add a fresh, light touch to your wraps. I love using grilled salmon or canned tuna mixed with a bit of mayo for a quick, protein-packed lunch.

Plant-Based Proteins: If you're vegetarian or vegan, there are plenty of plant-based options, such as beans, lentils, tofu, and tempeh. One of my favourite wraps is a black bean and quinoa combination, filled with avocado and salsa. It's both filling and packed with flavour.

Vegetables

Fresh vegetables add colour, texture, and essential nutrients to your wraps. Here are some great options to consider:

Leafy Greens: Spinach, kale, and mixed greens are fantastic additions, providing vitamins and minerals. I often add a handful of spinach to my wraps for an extra boost of nutrients.

Crunchy Veggies: Carrots, cucumbers, bell peppers, and radishes bring a satisfying crunch. Sliced bell peppers are a personal favourite of mine, adding both colour and sweetness.

Roasted or Grilled Vegetables: Roasting or grilling vegetables enhances their natural sweetness and adds depth to your wraps. I often use roasted zucchini and peppers for a Mediterranean-inspired wrap that pairs beautifully with feta cheese and tzatziki sauce.

Sauces and Spreads

A great sauce or spread can elevate your wrap from good to extraordinary. Here are some delicious options to consider:

Dressings: Ranch, Caesar, or balsamic vinaigrette can add a burst of flavour to your wraps. I frequently drizzle my wraps with a light vinaigrette for a refreshing touch.

Spreads: Hummus, guacamole, and tzatziki are fantastic spreads that can add creaminess and enhance the overall taste of your wrap. Hummus is one of my go-to spreads; I love its creamy texture and the way it complements fresh vegetables.

Salsas and Relishes: Fresh salsa, mango salsa, or even a spicy relish can add a kick to your wrap. I often make a simple tomato and onion salsa to top off my chicken wraps, adding a zesty flavour.

Herbs and Seasonings

Don't underestimate the power of herbs and seasonings to elevate your wraps. Fresh herbs like cilantro, basil, or parsley can brighten up your ingredients, while spices can enhance the overall flavour.

I often sprinkle a bit of smoked paprika or cumin in my wraps for added depth. Fresh basil in a Caprese wrap, paired with mozzarella and tomatoes, is an unbeatable combination.

Personal Experience with Wrap Essentials

As I reflect on my journey with wraps, I remember the early days of experimenting in the kitchen. I started with simple ingredients, gradually learning how to balance flavours and textures. Over time, I discovered my favourite combinations and developed a knack for creating wraps that delighted my family and friends.

For instance, I recall a family gathering where I set up a "build-your-own-wrap" station. I prepared an array of tortillas, lettuce leaves, and fillings, allowing everyone to create their own masterpiece. It was a hit! Guests enjoyed trying different combinations and sharing their creations with one another, illustrating how wraps can bring people together.

Conclusion

Understanding the essential components of wraps—types, key ingredients, and sauces—empowers you to create a diverse range of delicious meals. Whether you opt for a classic tortilla wrap, a refreshing lettuce leaf, or a unique rice paper roll, the possibilities are virtually endless.

As you explore the world of wraps, I encourage you to get creative with your combinations. Don't be afraid to experiment with different ingredients and flavours. The joy of wraps lies in their versatility, allowing you to tailor them to your personal tastes and dietary preferences. So roll up your sleeves, gather your ingredients, and let your imagination run wild as you embark on your wrap-making journey!

CHAPTER 1: BREAKFAST WRAPS

1. Spinach and Feta Egg Wrap

Prep: 10 mins | Cook: 10 mins | Serves: 2

Ingredients:

- US: 4 large eggs, 100g fresh spinach, 50g feta cheese (crumbled), 2 whole wheat tortillas, 15ml olive oil, salt, pepper
- UK: 4 large eggs, 100g fresh spinach, 50g feta cheese (crumbled), 2 whole wheat tortillas, 15ml olive oil, salt, pepper

Instructions:

1. In a bowl, whisk the eggs and season with salt and pepper.
2. Heat the olive oil in a frying pan over medium heat.
3. Add the spinach and sauté for 1-2 minutes until wilted.
4. Pour in the eggs and cook gently, stirring, until just set.
5. Remove from heat and crumble in the feta.
6. Spoon the mixture onto the tortillas, wrap tightly, and serve warm.

Calories: 350 | Fat: 20g | Carbs: 30g | Protein: 18g

2. Avocado and Bacon Breakfast Wrap

Prep: 5 mins | Cook: 5 mins | Serves: 2

Ingredients:

- US: 100g cooked bacon (sliced), 1 ripe avocado (sliced), 2 whole wheat tortillas, 30ml mayonnaise, 10g fresh cilantro (chopped), salt, pepper
- UK: 100g cooked bacon (sliced), 1 ripe avocado (sliced), 2 whole wheat tortillas, 30ml mayonnaise, 10g fresh coriander (chopped), salt, pepper

Instructions:

1. Spread mayonnaise on each tortilla.
2. Layer the sliced avocado and bacon on top.
3. Sprinkle with cilantro, salt, and pepper.
4. Roll the tortilla tightly and slice in half to serve.

Calories: 450 | Fat: 28g | Carbs: 35g | Protein: 15g

3. Berry Yogurt and Granola Wrap

Prep: 5 mins | Cook: 0 mins | Serves: 2

Ingredients:

- US: 200g Greek yogurt, 100g mixed berries, 50g granola, 2 whole wheat tortillas, honey (to taste)
- UK: 200g Greek yogurt, 100g mixed berries, 50g granola, 2 whole wheat tortillas, honey (to taste)

Instructions:

1. Spread Greek yogurt evenly over each tortilla.
2. Top with mixed berries and granola.
3. Drizzle with honey, if desired.
4. Roll up tightly and slice to serve.

Calories: 300 | Fat: 7g | Carbs: 40g | Protein: 15g

4. Scrambled Tofu and Veggie Wrap

Prep: 10 mins | Cook: 10 mins | Serves: 2

Ingredients:

- US: 200g firm tofu (crumbled), 100g mixed bell peppers (chopped), 50g onion (chopped), 2 whole wheat tortillas, 15ml olive oil, salt, pepper
- UK: 200g firm tofu (crumbled), 100g mixed bell peppers (chopped), 50g onion (chopped), 2 whole wheat tortillas, 15ml olive oil, salt, pepper

Instructions:

1. Heat olive oil in a frying pan over medium heat.
2. Sauté the onion and bell peppers for 3-4 minutes.
3. Add crumbled tofu, seasoning with salt and pepper, and cook for another 5 minutes.

4. Spoon the mixture onto tortillas, roll them up, and serve warm.

Calories: 400 | Fat: 20g | Carbs: 30g | Protein: 25g

5. Peanut Butter Banana Wrap

Prep: 5 mins | Cook: 0 mins | Serves: 1

Ingredients:

- US: 2 tablespoons peanut butter, 1 ripe banana (sliced), 1 whole wheat tortilla, honey (optional)
- UK: 2 tablespoons peanut butter, 1 ripe banana (sliced), 1 whole wheat tortilla, honey (optional)

Instructions:

1. Spread peanut butter evenly on the tortilla.
2. Lay the banana slices on top.
3. Drizzle with honey, if desired.
4. Roll up the tortilla tightly and enjoy.

Calories: 350 | Fat: 16g | Carbs: 40g | Protein: 10g

6. Smoked Salmon and Cream Cheese Wrap

Prep: 5 mins | Cook: 0 mins | Serves: 2

Ingredients:

- US: 100g smoked salmon, 50g cream cheese, 2 whole wheat tortillas, capers (to taste), fresh dill (for garnish)
- UK: 100g smoked salmon, 50g cream cheese, 2 whole wheat tortillas, capers (to taste), fresh dill (for garnish)

Instructions:

1. Spread cream cheese on each tortilla.
2. Layer the smoked salmon, capers, and dill on top.
3. Roll tightly and slice to serve.

Calories: 300 | Fat: 18g | Carbs: 25g | Protein: 20g

7. Veggie Omelette Wrap

Prep: 10 mins | Cook: 10 mins | Serves: 2

Ingredients:

- US: 4 large eggs, 100g mixed vegetables (chopped), 2 whole wheat tortillas, 15ml olive oil, salt, pepper
- UK: 4 large eggs, 100g mixed vegetables (chopped), 2 whole wheat tortillas, 15ml olive oil, salt, pepper

Instructions:

1. In a bowl, whisk the eggs with salt and pepper.
2. Heat olive oil in a pan over medium heat.
3. Add the mixed vegetables and sauté for 3-4 minutes.
4. Pour in the eggs and cook until set, then fold.
5. Spoon onto tortillas, wrap, and serve.

Calories: 350 | Fat: 20g | Carbs: 30g | Protein: 18g

8. Breakfast Burrito Wrap

Prep: 10 mins | Cook: 15 mins | Serves: 2

Ingredients:

- US: 4 large eggs, 100g cooked sausage (crumbled), 50g shredded cheese, 2 large flour tortillas, salsa (to serve)
- UK: 4 large eggs, 100g cooked sausage (crumbled), 50g shredded cheese, 2 large flour tortillas, salsa (to serve)

Instructions:

1. In a bowl, whisk eggs and cook in a pan until scrambled.
2. Stir in the crumbled sausage and cheese until melted.
3. Spoon the mixture onto tortillas, roll up, and serve with salsa.

Calories: 500 | Fat: 30g | Carbs: 40g | Protein: 25g

9. Chia Seed Pudding Wrap

Prep: 10 mins | Cook: 0 mins | Serves: 2

Ingredients:

- US: 100g chia seeds, 400ml almond milk, 30ml maple syrup, 2 whole wheat tortillas, mixed berries (for topping)
- UK: 100g chia seeds, 400ml almond milk, 30ml maple syrup, 2 whole wheat tortillas, mixed berries (for topping)

Instructions:

1. Mix chia seeds, almond milk, and maple syrup in a bowl.
2. Refrigerate for at least 2 hours until thickened.
3. Spoon the pudding onto tortillas, top with berries, roll up, and serve.

Calories: 350 | Fat: 15g | Carbs: 40g | Protein: 10g

10. Sweet Potato and Black Bean Wrap

Prep: 15 mins | Cook: 20 mins | Serves: 2

Ingredients:

- US: 200g sweet potato (cubed), 100g canned black beans (drained), 2 whole wheat tortillas, 15ml olive oil, cumin (to taste), salt, pepper
- UK: 200g sweet potato (cubed), 100g canned black beans (drained), 2 whole wheat tortillas, 15ml olive oil, cumin (to taste), salt, pepper

Instructions:

1. Boil sweet potatoes until tender, about 15 minutes.
2. Drain and mash with olive oil, cumin, salt, and pepper.
3. Spread the mixture onto tortillas, add black beans, roll up, and serve.

Calories: 400 | Fat: 10g | Carbs: 65g | Protein: 15g

CHAPTER 2: LUNCH WRAPS

1. Turkey and Hummus Wrap

Prep: 10 mins | Cook: 0 mins | Serves: 2

Ingredients:

- US: 200g sliced turkey breast, 100g hummus, 100g mixed greens, 50g sliced cucumber, 50g shredded carrots, 2 large whole wheat wraps
- UK: 200g sliced turkey breast, 100g hummus, 100g mixed greens, 50g sliced cucumber, 50g shredded carrots, 2 large whole wheat wraps

Instructions:

1. Spread a generous layer of hummus on each wrap.
2. Layer the sliced turkey, mixed greens, cucumber, and shredded carrots on top.
3. Roll the wrap tightly, folding in the sides as you go.
4. Slice in half and serve with your favourite dipping sauce.

Nutritional Info: Calories: 350 | Fat: 10g | Carbs: 40g | Protein: 25g

2. Mediterranean Veggie Wrap

Prep: 15 mins | Cook: 0 mins | Serves: 2

Ingredients:

- US: 100g roasted red peppers, 100g feta cheese, 100g spinach, 50g cucumber, 50g olives, 2 large spinach wraps
- UK: 100g roasted red peppers, 100g feta cheese, 100g spinach, 50g cucumber, 50g olives, 2 large spinach wraps

Instructions:

1. Spread the roasted red peppers evenly over each wrap.
2. Crumble feta cheese on top, then add spinach, cucumber, and olives.
3. Tightly roll the wraps, ensuring the filling stays inside.
4. Cut in half and enjoy!

Nutritional Info: Calories: 300 | Fat: 15g | Carbs: 30g | Protein: 10g

3. Chicken Caesar Salad Wrap

Prep: 10 mins | Cook: 10 mins | Serves: 2

Ingredients:

- US: 200g cooked chicken breast (sliced), 50g Caesar dressing, 50g romaine lettuce, 30g Parmesan cheese, 2 large flour tortillas
- UK: 200g cooked chicken breast (sliced), 50g Caesar dressing, 50g romaine lettuce, 30g Parmesan cheese, 2 large flour tortillas

Instructions:

1. In a bowl, mix the sliced chicken with Caesar dressing.
2. Lay the romaine lettuce on each tortilla, followed by the chicken mixture and Parmesan.
3. Roll the tortillas tightly, folding in the ends.
4. Slice in half and serve with extra dressing if desired.

Nutritional Info: Calories: 450 | Fat: 20g | Carbs: 30g | Protein: 35g

4. BBQ Pulled Pork Wrap

Prep: 15 mins | Cook: 1 hour | Serves: 2

Ingredients:

- US: 300g pulled pork, 50g BBQ sauce, 100g coleslaw, 2 large tortilla wraps
- UK: 300g pulled pork, 50g BBQ sauce, 100g coleslaw, 2 large tortilla wraps

Instructions:

1. Mix the pulled pork with BBQ sauce in a bowl until coated.
2. Spread coleslaw evenly over each wrap.
3. Add the BBQ pork on top of the coleslaw.
4. Roll the wraps tightly, cut in half, and dig in!

Nutritional Info: Calories: 600 | Fat: 25g | Carbs: 50g | Protein: 40g

5. Caprese Wrap with Pesto

Prep: 10 mins | Cook: 0 mins | Serves: 2

Ingredients:

- US: 100g mozzarella cheese (sliced), 100g fresh tomatoes (sliced), 50g fresh basil, 50g pesto, 2 large wraps
- UK: 100g mozzarella cheese (sliced), 100g fresh tomatoes (sliced), 50g fresh basil, 50g pesto, 2 large wraps

Instructions:

1. Spread pesto evenly over each wrap.
2. Layer mozzarella, tomatoes, and basil on top.
3. Roll tightly, making sure the filling is secure.
4. Slice in half and serve fresh!

Nutritional Info: Calories: 400 | Fat: 25g | Carbs: 30g | Protein: 15g

6. Quinoa and Roasted Veggie Wrap

Prep: 15 mins | Cook: 30 mins | Serves: 2

Ingredients:

- US: 150g cooked quinoa, 100g roasted vegetables (zucchini, bell peppers, etc.), 50g hummus, 2 large whole grain wraps
- UK: 150g cooked quinoa, 100g roasted vegetables (zucchini, bell peppers, etc.), 50g hummus, 2 large whole grain wraps

Instructions:

1. Spread hummus on each wrap.
2. Add cooked quinoa and roasted veggies on top.
3. Roll tightly and slice in half for a hearty meal.
4. Enjoy cold or warm!

Nutritional Info: Calories: 350 | Fat: 8g | Carbs: 55g | Protein: 12g

7. Tuna Salad Wrap

Prep: 10 mins | Cook: 0 mins | Serves: 2

Ingredients:

- US: 200g canned tuna (drained), 50g mayonnaise, 50g diced celery, 50g diced red onion, 2 large wraps
- UK: 200g canned tuna (drained), 50g mayonnaise, 50g diced celery, 50g diced red onion, 2 large wraps

Instructions:

1. In a bowl, combine tuna, mayonnaise, celery, and red onion.
2. Spread the mixture evenly on each wrap.
3. Roll tightly and cut in half.
4. Serve with a side of crisps or salad.

Nutritional Info: Calories: 300 | Fat: 15g | Carbs: 20g | Protein: 25g

8. Greek Chicken Wrap

Prep: 10 mins | Cook: 10 mins | Serves: 2

Ingredients:

- US: 200g cooked chicken (sliced), 50g tzatziki sauce, 50g cucumber (sliced), 50g tomatoes (diced), 2 large pitta wraps
- UK: 200g cooked chicken (sliced), 50g tzatziki sauce, 50g cucumber (sliced), 50g tomatoes (diced), 2 large pitta wraps

Instructions:

1. Spread tzatziki on each pitta.
2. Layer the chicken, cucumber, and tomatoes.
3. Roll up the pitta tightly.
4. Slice and serve with extra tzatziki if desired.

Nutritional Info: Calories: 400 | Fat: 12g | Carbs: 35g | Protein: 30g

9. Falafel and Tzatziki Wrap

Prep: 10 mins | Cook: 15 mins | Serves: 2

Ingredients:

- US: 200g cooked falafel, 50g tzatziki sauce, 100g mixed greens, 2 large wraps
- UK: 200g cooked falafel, 50g tzatziki sauce, 100g mixed greens, 2 large wraps

Instructions:

1. Spread tzatziki on each wrap.
2. Add mixed greens and falafel on top.
3. Roll tightly and cut in half.
4. Serve with a side of salad.

Nutritional Info: Calories: 450 | Fat: 20g | Carbs: 50g | Protein: 15g

10. Cucumber and Cream Cheese Wrap

Prep: 10 mins | Cook: 0 mins | Serves: 2

Ingredients:

- US: 100g cream cheese, 100g cucumber (sliced), 50g smoked salmon (optional), 2 large wraps
- UK: 100g cream cheese, 100g cucumber (sliced), 50g smoked salmon (optional), 2 large wraps

Instructions:

1. Spread cream cheese evenly on each wrap.
2. Layer cucumber slices and smoked salmon if using.
3. Roll tightly, slice, and serve.
4. Perfect for a light lunch!

Nutritional Info: Calories: 300 | Fat: 20g | Carbs: 25g | Protein: 10g

CHAPTER 3: DINNER WRAPS

1. Teriyaki Chicken Wrap

Prep: 10 mins | Cook: 15 mins | Serves: 2

Ingredients:

- US: 200g cooked chicken (shredded), 50ml teriyaki sauce, 100g mixed salad greens, 2 flour tortillas, 10g sesame seeds
- UK: 200g cooked chicken (shredded), 50ml teriyaki sauce, 100g mixed salad greens, 2 flour tortillas, 10g sesame seeds

Instructions:

1. In a bowl, mix the shredded chicken with teriyaki sauce until coated.
2. Warm the tortillas slightly in a pan.
3. Lay the salad greens on each tortilla.
4. Top with the teriyaki chicken and sprinkle with sesame seeds.
5. Roll up tightly and slice in half to serve.

Calories: 450 | Fat: 15g | Carbs: 45g | Protein: 30g

2. Beef and Broccoli Wrap

Prep: 10 mins | Cook: 15 mins | Serves: 2

Ingredients:

- US: 200g beef (thinly sliced), 100g broccoli florets, 50ml soy sauce, 2 flour tortillas, 15ml olive oil, garlic (to taste)
- UK: 200g beef (thinly sliced), 100g broccoli florets, 50ml soy sauce, 2 flour tortillas, 15ml olive oil, garlic (to taste)

Instructions:

1. Heat olive oil in a pan over medium-high heat.
2. Add garlic and sauté for a minute before adding beef.
3. Cook beef for 5 minutes, then add broccoli and soy sauce.

4. Stir-fry until broccoli is tender.
5. Spoon the mixture onto tortillas, wrap, and serve.

Calories: 500 | Fat: 25g | Carbs: 30g | Protein: 35g

3. Shrimp Taco Wrap

Prep: 10 mins | Cook: 10 mins | Serves: 2

Ingredients:

- US: 200g shrimp (peeled and deveined), 1 teaspoon cumin, 2 flour tortillas, 50g shredded cabbage, 30ml lime juice, 10g fresh cilantro
- UK: 200g shrimp (peeled and deveined), 1 teaspoon cumin, 2 flour tortillas, 50g shredded cabbage, 30ml lime juice, 10g fresh coriander

Instructions:

1. In a bowl, toss shrimp with cumin, lime juice, salt, and pepper.
2. Cook shrimp in a pan over medium heat for 5-7 minutes until pink.
3. Warm tortillas and add shredded cabbage.
4. Top with shrimp and garnish with cilantro before rolling up.

Calories: 350 | Fat: 10g | Carbs: 30g | Protein: 30g

4. Vegetarian Stir-Fry Wrap

Prep: 10 mins | Cook: 10 mins | Serves: 2

Ingredients:

- US: 150g mixed vegetables (bell peppers, carrots, snap peas), 100g tofu (cubed), 50ml soy sauce, 2 flour tortillas, 15ml olive oil
- UK: 150g mixed vegetables (bell peppers, carrots, snap peas), 100g tofu (cubed), 50ml soy sauce, 2 flour tortillas, 15ml olive oil

Instructions:

1. Heat olive oil in a pan over medium heat.
2. Add tofu and fry until golden.
3. Toss in mixed vegetables and stir-fry for about 5 minutes.
4. Add soy sauce and cook for another minute.

5. Spoon into tortillas, wrap, and serve.

Calories: 400 | Fat: 20g | Carbs: 35g | Protein: 15g

5. Chicken Fajita Wrap

Prep: 10 mins | Cook: 10 mins | Serves: 2

Ingredients:

- US: 200g cooked chicken (sliced), 100g bell peppers (sliced), 50g onion (sliced), 2 flour tortillas, 10ml fajita seasoning, 15ml olive oil
- UK: 200g cooked chicken (sliced), 100g bell peppers (sliced), 50g onion (sliced), 2 flour tortillas, 10ml fajita seasoning, 15ml olive oil

Instructions:

1. Heat olive oil in a frying pan and sauté onions and bell peppers until softened.
2. Add chicken and fajita seasoning, cooking for another 5 minutes.
3. Warm tortillas and fill with the chicken mixture.
4. Roll up and serve warm.

Calories: 450 | Fat: 18g | Carbs: 40g | Protein: 30g

6. Pesto Pasta and Chicken Wrap

Prep: 10 mins | Cook: 15 mins | Serves: 2

Ingredients:

- US: 200g cooked pasta, 150g cooked chicken (sliced), 30ml pesto, 2 flour tortillas, 10g grated Parmesan cheese
- UK: 200g cooked pasta, 150g cooked chicken (sliced), 30ml pesto, 2 flour tortillas, 10g grated Parmesan cheese

Instructions:

1. In a bowl, mix cooked pasta with chicken and pesto.
2. Spread the mixture onto each tortilla.
3. Sprinkle with Parmesan cheese and roll up tightly.
4. Serve cold or warm.

Calories: 600 | Fat: 25g | Carbs: 60g | Protein: 35g

7. Moroccan Spiced Lamb Wrap

Prep: 10 mins | Cook: 15 mins | Serves: 2

Ingredients:

- US: 200g cooked lamb (shredded), 1 teaspoon Moroccan spice blend, 100g mixed salad greens, 2 flour tortillas, 30ml tzatziki sauce
- UK: 200g cooked lamb (shredded), 1 teaspoon Moroccan spice blend, 100g mixed salad greens, 2 flour tortillas, 30ml tzatziki sauce

Instructions:

1. In a bowl, mix shredded lamb with Moroccan spices.
2. Warm tortillas in a pan.
3. Layer salad greens on each tortilla, then add spiced lamb.
4. Drizzle with tzatziki, wrap up, and serve.

Calories: 500 | Fat: 25g | Carbs: 35g | Protein: 30g

8. Stuffed Bell Pepper Wrap

Prep: 15 mins | Cook: 20 mins | Serves: 2

Ingredients:

- US: 2 bell peppers (halved), 150g cooked rice, 100g black beans (drained), 50g cheese (shredded), 2 flour tortillas
- UK: 2 bell peppers (halved), 150g cooked rice, 100g black beans (drained), 50g cheese (shredded), 2 flour tortillas

Instructions:

1. Preheat oven to 180°C.
2. Mix rice, black beans, and cheese in a bowl.
3. Fill each bell pepper half with the mixture.
4. Bake for 15-20 minutes until peppers are tender.
5. Place the stuffed peppers on tortillas, roll up, and serve.

Calories: 400 | Fat: 15g | Carbs: 50g | Protein: 15g

9. Coconut Curry Chicken Wrap

Prep: 10 mins | Cook: 15 mins | Serves: 2

Ingredients:

- US: 200g cooked chicken (shredded), 100ml coconut milk, 20g curry paste, 2 flour tortillas, 100g mixed salad greens
- UK: 200g cooked chicken (shredded), 100ml coconut milk, 20g curry paste, 2 flour tortillas, 100g mixed salad greens

Instructions:

1. In a pan, combine coconut milk and curry paste over medium heat.
2. Stir in shredded chicken and cook until heated through.
3. Warm tortillas and layer with salad greens.
4. Top with curry chicken, roll up, and serve.

Calories: 500 | Fat: 28g | Carbs: 35g | Protein: 30g

10. Moussaka Wrap

Prep: 15 mins | Cook: 30 mins | Serves: 2

Ingredients:

- US: 200g cooked minced lamb, 100g eggplant (sliced and grilled), 50g béchamel sauce, 2 flour tortillas, 10g grated cheese
- UK: 200g cooked minced lamb, 100g eggplant (sliced and grilled), 50g béchamel sauce, 2 flour tortillas, 10g grated cheese

Instructions:

1. In a pan, heat the minced lamb until warm.
2. Layer grilled eggplant on each tortilla, followed by lamb and béchamel sauce.
3. Sprinkle with cheese and roll up tightly.
4. Serve warm for a hearty dinner option.

Calories: 600 | Fat: 35g | Carbs: 40g | Protein: 30g

CHAPTER 4: SNACK WRAPS

1. Cheese and Apple Wrap

Prep: 5 mins | Cook: 0 mins | Serves: 2

Ingredients:

- US: 100g cheese (cheddar or your choice), 1 large apple (sliced), 2 large whole wheat wraps
- UK: 100g cheese (cheddar or your choice), 1 large apple (sliced), 2 large whole wheat wraps

Instructions:

1. Lay the cheese slices on each wrap.
2. Top with apple slices, arranging them evenly.
3. Roll the wrap tightly, folding in the ends.
4. Slice in half and enjoy a sweet and savory snack!

Nutritional Info: Calories: 250 | Fat: 15g | Carbs: 25g | Protein: 10g

2. Veggie Sticks and Hummus Wrap

Prep: 10 mins | Cook: 0 mins | Serves: 2

Ingredients:

- US: 100g assorted veggie sticks (carrots, cucumber, bell peppers), 100g hummus, 2 large wraps
- UK: 100g assorted veggie sticks (carrots, cucumber, bell peppers), 100g hummus, 2 large wraps

Instructions:

1. Spread hummus evenly over each wrap.
2. Arrange the veggie sticks on top.
3. Roll tightly, ensuring the veggies stay in.
4. Slice in half and enjoy your crunchy snack!

Nutritional Info: Calories: 200 | Fat: 8g | Carbs: 30g | Protein: 6g

3. Nut Butter and Fruit Wrap

Prep: 5 mins | Cook: 0 mins | Serves: 2

Ingredients:

- US: 100g nut butter (peanut or almond), 1 large banana (sliced), 2 large wraps
- UK: 100g nut butter (peanut or almond), 1 large banana (sliced), 2 large wraps

Instructions:

1. Spread the nut butter on each wrap.
2. Add banana slices on top of the nut butter.
3. Roll the wraps tightly and cut in half.
4. Enjoy a protein-packed snack!

Nutritional Info: Calories: 400 | Fat: 20g | Carbs: 40g | Protein: 15g

4. Popcorn and Cheddar Wrap

Prep: 5 mins | Cook: 0 mins | Serves: 2

Ingredients:

- US: 50g popcorn (popped), 100g cheddar cheese (shredded), 2 large wraps
- UK: 50g popcorn (popped), 100g cheddar cheese (shredded), 2 large wraps

Instructions:

1. Lay the popcorn on each wrap.
2. Sprinkle the shredded cheddar on top.
3. Roll the wrap tightly and slice in half.
4. Enjoy this crunchy, cheesy delight!

Nutritional Info: Calories: 350 | Fat: 18g | Carbs: 30g | Protein: 12g

5. Antipasto Skewers Wrap

Prep: 10 mins | Cook: 0 mins | Serves: 2

Ingredients:

- US: 100g assorted antipasto (olives, salami, cheese), 50g balsamic glaze, 2 large wraps
- UK: 100g assorted antipasto (olives, salami, cheese), 50g balsamic glaze, 2 large wraps

Instructions:

1. Arrange antipasto on each wrap.
2. Drizzle with balsamic glaze.
3. Roll tightly and cut in half.
4. Perfect for a quick and flavorful snack!

Nutritional Info: Calories: 400 | Fat: 30g | Carbs: 15g | Protein: 20g

6. Sweet and Savory Trail Mix Wrap

Prep: 5 mins | Cook: 0 mins | Serves: 2

Ingredients:

- US: 100g trail mix (nuts, dried fruit, chocolate), 50g yogurt, 2 large wraps
- UK: 100g trail mix (nuts, dried fruit, chocolate), 50g yogurt, 2 large wraps

Instructions:

1. Spread yogurt over each wrap.
2. Sprinkle trail mix evenly on top.
3. Roll tightly and slice in half.
4. Enjoy a delightful mix of sweet and savory!

Nutritional Info: Calories: 350 | Fat: 15g | Carbs: 40g | Protein: 10g

7. Energy Bar Wrap

Prep: 5 mins | Cook: 0 mins | Serves: 2

Ingredients:

- US: 100g energy bar (chopped), 100g banana (sliced), 2 large wraps
- UK: 100g energy bar (chopped), 100g banana (sliced), 2 large wraps

Instructions:

1. Lay the chopped energy bar on each wrap.
2. Add banana slices on top.
3. Roll tightly and cut in half.
4. A perfect snack to fuel your day!

Nutritional Info: Calories: 400 | Fat: 15g | Carbs: 55g | Protein: 10g

8. Salsa and Guacamole Wrap

Prep: 10 mins | Cook: 0 mins | Serves: 2

Ingredients:

- US: 100g salsa, 100g guacamole, 2 large wraps
- UK: 100g salsa, 100g guacamole, 2 large wraps

Instructions:

1. Spread salsa evenly over each wrap.
2. Top with guacamole.
3. Roll tightly and slice in half.
4. Enjoy this zesty snack!

Nutritional Info: Calories: 300 | Fat: 20g | Carbs: 30g | Protein: 5g

9. Chocolate Banana Wrap

Prep: 5 mins | Cook: 0 mins | Serves: 2

Ingredients:

- US: 100g chocolate spread, 1 large banana (sliced), 2 large wraps
- UK: 100g chocolate spread, 1 large banana (sliced), 2 large wraps

Instructions:

1. Spread chocolate spread evenly on each wrap.
2. Add banana slices on top.
3. Roll tightly and slice in half.
4. Treat yourself to a sweet snack!

Nutritional Info: Calories: 450 | Fat: 20g | Carbs: 60g | Protein: 6g

10. Crispy Chickpea Wrap

Prep: 10 mins | Cook: 20 mins | Serves: 2

Ingredients:

- US: 200g canned chickpeas (drained and rinsed), 50g olive oil, 1 teaspoon smoked paprika, 2 large wraps
- UK: 200g canned chickpeas (drained and rinsed), 50g olive oil, 1 teaspoon smoked paprika, 2 large wraps

Instructions:

1. Preheat your oven to 200°C (400°F).
2. Toss chickpeas with olive oil and smoked paprika.
3. Spread on a baking tray and roast for 20 minutes until crispy.
4. Lay crispy chickpeas on each wrap and roll tightly.
5. Slice and enjoy a crunchy snack!

Nutritional Info: Calories: 350 | Fat: 15g | Carbs: 40g | Protein: 12g

CHAPTER 5: VEGETARIAN WRAPS

1. Roasted Vegetable Wrap

Prep: 10 mins | Cook: 20 mins | Serves: 2

Ingredients:

- US: 200g mixed vegetables (bell peppers, zucchini, onion), 15ml olive oil, 2 whole wheat tortillas, 50g hummus, salt, pepper
- UK: 200g mixed vegetables (bell peppers, zucchini, onion), 15ml olive oil, 2 whole wheat tortillas, 50g hummus, salt, pepper

Instructions:

1. Preheat the oven to 200°C.
2. Toss the mixed vegetables with olive oil, salt, and pepper.
3. Spread on a baking tray and roast for 20 minutes.
4. Spread hummus on each tortilla, add roasted vegetables, and roll up tightly.

Calories: 350 | Fat: 12g | Carbs: 45g | Protein: 10g

2. Spicy Black Bean Wrap

Prep: 5 mins | Cook: 5 mins | Serves: 2

Ingredients:

- US: 200g canned black beans (drained), 1 teaspoon chili powder, 2 whole wheat tortillas, 50g avocado (sliced), 15ml lime juice
- UK: 200g canned black beans (drained), 1 teaspoon chili powder, 2 whole wheat tortillas, 50g avocado (sliced), 15ml lime juice

Instructions:

1. In a bowl, mash black beans with chili powder and lime juice.
2. Spread the mixture on each tortilla.
3. Top with sliced avocado and roll up tightly.

Calories: 400 | Fat: 15g | Carbs: 55g | Protein: 18g

3. Lentil Salad Wrap

Prep: 10 mins | Cook: 10 mins | Serves: 2

Ingredients:

- US: 150g cooked lentils, 50g cherry tomatoes (halved), 50g cucumber (diced), 2 whole wheat tortillas, 30ml balsamic vinaigrette
- UK: 150g cooked lentils, 50g cherry tomatoes (halved), 50g cucumber (diced), 2 whole wheat tortillas, 30ml balsamic vinaigrette

Instructions:

1. In a bowl, mix lentils, cherry tomatoes, cucumber, and vinaigrette.
2. Spoon the salad onto each tortilla.
3. Roll up and serve cold or at room temperature.

Calories: 350 | Fat: 5g | Carbs: 55g | Protein: 20g

4. Grilled Eggplant and Zucchini Wrap

Prep: 10 mins | Cook: 15 mins | Serves: 2

Ingredients:

- US: 100g eggplant (sliced), 100g zucchini (sliced), 15ml olive oil, 2 whole wheat tortillas, 50g feta cheese (crumbled), salt, pepper
- UK: 100g eggplant (sliced), 100g zucchini (sliced), 15ml olive oil, 2 whole wheat tortillas, 50g feta cheese (crumbled), salt, pepper

Instructions:

1. Heat olive oil in a grill pan over medium heat.
2. Grill eggplant and zucchini slices for 4-5 minutes on each side.
3. Place grilled vegetables on tortillas, sprinkle with feta, and roll up.

Calories: 400 | Fat: 20g | Carbs: 35g | Protein: 15g

5. Chickpea Salad Wrap

Prep: 10 mins | Cook: 0 mins | Serves: 2

Ingredients:

- US: 200g canned chickpeas (drained), 50g red onion (diced), 50g cucumber (diced), 30ml olive oil, 2 whole wheat tortillas, lemon juice (to taste)
- UK: 200g canned chickpeas (drained), 50g red onion (diced), 50g cucumber (diced), 30ml olive oil, 2 whole wheat tortillas, lemon juice (to taste)

Instructions:

1. In a bowl, mix chickpeas, onion, cucumber, olive oil, and lemon juice.
2. Spread the mixture on tortillas and roll up tightly.

Calories: 450 | Fat: 15g | Carbs: 60g | Protein: 20g

6. Caprese Pesto Wrap

Prep: 5 mins | Cook: 0 mins | Serves: 2

Ingredients:

- US: 100g mozzarella cheese (sliced), 100g tomatoes (sliced), 30ml pesto, 2 whole wheat tortillas, fresh basil leaves
- UK: 100g mozzarella cheese (sliced), 100g tomatoes (sliced), 30ml pesto, 2 whole wheat tortillas, fresh basil leaves

Instructions:

1. Spread pesto on each tortilla.
2. Layer mozzarella, tomatoes, and basil leaves.
3. Roll up tightly and slice to serve.

Calories: 350 | Fat: 22g | Carbs: 25g | Protein: 15g

7. Stuffed Portobello Mushroom Wrap

Prep: 10 mins | Cook: 15 mins | Serves: 2

Ingredients:

- US: 2 large portobello mushrooms, 100g spinach, 50g cream cheese, 2 whole wheat tortillas, 15ml olive oil
- UK: 2 large portobello mushrooms, 100g spinach, 50g cream cheese, 2 whole wheat tortillas, 15ml olive oil

Instructions:

1. Preheat oven to 200°C.
2. Sauté spinach in olive oil until wilted.
3. Mix with cream cheese and fill each mushroom cap.
4. Bake for 10 minutes, then place on tortillas, wrap, and serve.

Calories: 400 | Fat: 25g | Carbs: 30g | Protein: 15g

8. Ratatouille Wrap

Prep: 15 mins | Cook: 20 mins | Serves: 2

Ingredients:

- US: 100g zucchini (diced), 100g eggplant (diced), 100g bell peppers (diced), 2 whole wheat tortillas, 15ml olive oil, herbs de Provence
- UK: 100g zucchini (diced), 100g eggplant (diced), 100g bell peppers (diced), 2 whole wheat tortillas, 15ml olive oil, herbs de Provence

Instructions:

1. Heat olive oil in a pan and sauté vegetables with herbs until tender.
2. Spoon ratatouille onto each tortilla and roll up tightly.

Calories: 350 | Fat: 10g | Carbs: 45g | Protein: 10g

9. Curried Cauliflower Wrap

Prep: 10 mins | Cook: 20 mins | Serves: 2

Ingredients:

- US: 200g cauliflower florets, 15ml curry powder, 15ml olive oil, 2 whole wheat tortillas, 50g yogurt (for topping)
- UK: 200g cauliflower florets, 15ml curry powder, 15ml olive oil, 2 whole wheat tortillas, 50g yogurt (for topping)

Instructions:

1. Preheat oven to 200°C.
2. Toss cauliflower with olive oil and curry powder.
3. Roast for 20 minutes until tender.
4. Fill tortillas with roasted cauliflower and top with yogurt.

Calories: 400 | Fat: 15g | Carbs: 50g | Protein: 12g

10. Spinach and Ricotta Wrap

Prep: 5 mins | Cook: 5 mins | Serves: 2

Ingredients:

- US: 100g ricotta cheese, 100g fresh spinach, 2 whole wheat tortillas, 15ml olive oil, salt, pepper
- UK: 100g ricotta cheese, 100g fresh spinach, 2 whole wheat tortillas, 15ml olive oil, salt, pepper

Instructions:

1. In a pan, heat olive oil and sauté spinach until wilted.
2. Mix spinach with ricotta, salt, and pepper.
3. Spread the mixture on tortillas, roll up, and serve.

Calories: 300 | Fat: 15g | Carbs: 25g | Protein: 12g

CHAPTER 6: VEGAN WRAPS

1. Tofu and Vegetable Stir-Fry Wrap

Prep: 15 mins | Cook: 10 mins | Serves: 2

Ingredients:

- US: 200g firm tofu (cubed), 150g mixed vegetables (bell peppers, broccoli, carrots), 30ml soy sauce, 2 large wraps
- UK: 200g firm tofu (cubed), 150g mixed vegetables (bell peppers, broccoli, carrots), 30ml soy sauce, 2 large wraps

Instructions:

1. Heat a non-stick pan over medium heat and sauté tofu until golden brown.
2. Add mixed vegetables and soy sauce, stirring for about 5-7 minutes until tender.
3. Lay the stir-fry mixture on each wrap.
4. Roll tightly and cut in half to serve.

Nutritional Info: Calories: 350 | Fat: 20g | Carbs: 30g | Protein: 15g

2. Roasted Beet and Avocado Wrap

Prep: 10 mins | Cook: 30 mins | Serves: 2

Ingredients:

- US: 150g roasted beets (sliced), 1 ripe avocado (sliced), 50g mixed greens, 2 large whole grain wraps
- UK: 150g roasted beets (sliced), 1 ripe avocado (sliced), 50g mixed greens, 2 large whole grain wraps

Instructions:

1. Preheat your oven to 200°C (400°F) and roast beets for about 30 minutes until tender.
2. Spread sliced avocado on each wrap.
3. Layer with roasted beets and mixed greens.
4. Roll tightly and slice to serve.

Nutritional Info: Calories: 400 | Fat: 25g | Carbs: 35g | Protein: 8g

3. Chickpea and Avocado Mash Wrap

Prep: 10 mins | Cook: 0 mins | Serves: 2

Ingredients:

- US: 200g canned chickpeas (drained), 1 ripe avocado, 50g lime juice, 2 large wraps
- UK: 200g canned chickpeas (drained), 1 ripe avocado, 50g lime juice, 2 large wraps

Instructions:

1. In a bowl, mash chickpeas and avocado together with lime juice until combined.
2. Spread the mixture onto each wrap.
3. Roll tightly and slice in half.
4. Enjoy this creamy and filling snack!

Nutritional Info: Calories: 300 | Fat: 15g | Carbs: 30g | Protein: 10g

4. Vegan BBQ Jackfruit Wrap

Prep: 15 mins | Cook: 20 mins | Serves: 2

Ingredients:

- US: 200g young green jackfruit (canned), 100g BBQ sauce, 50g coleslaw mix, 2 large wraps
- UK: 200g young green jackfruit (canned), 100g BBQ sauce, 50g coleslaw mix, 2 large wraps

Instructions:

1. Drain and rinse jackfruit, then shred it with a fork.
2. In a pan, cook jackfruit with BBQ sauce for about 10 minutes.
3. Lay the BBQ jackfruit on each wrap and top with coleslaw mix.
4. Roll tightly and cut in half.

Nutritional Info: Calories: 350 | Fat: 10g | Carbs: 50g | Protein: 15g

5. Sweet Potato and Kale Wrap

Prep: 10 mins | Cook: 30 mins | Serves: 2

Ingredients:

- US: 200g sweet potato (cubed), 100g kale (chopped), 30ml olive oil, 2 large wraps
- UK: 200g sweet potato (cubed), 100g kale (chopped), 30ml olive oil, 2 large wraps

Instructions:

1. Preheat oven to 200°C (400°F) and roast sweet potato for about 25 minutes.
2. Sauté kale in olive oil until wilted.
3. Combine roasted sweet potato and kale on each wrap.
4. Roll tightly and slice to serve.

Nutritional Info: Calories: 400 | Fat: 15g | Carbs: 60g | Protein: 8g

6. Thai Peanut Tofu Wrap

Prep: 15 mins | Cook: 10 mins | Serves: 2

Ingredients:

- US: 200g firm tofu (cubed), 50g peanut butter, 30ml soy sauce, 100g shredded carrots, 2 large wraps
- UK: 200g firm tofu (cubed), 50g peanut butter, 30ml soy sauce, 100g shredded carrots, 2 large wraps

Instructions:

1. Sauté tofu in a pan until golden brown.
2. Mix peanut butter and soy sauce, then toss with sautéed tofu and shredded carrots.
3. Spread the mixture on each wrap.
4. Roll tightly and enjoy!

Nutritional Info: Calories: 450 | Fat: 25g | Carbs: 30g | Protein: 20g

7. Zucchini Noodle Wrap

Prep: 10 mins | Cook: 0 mins | Serves: 2

Ingredients:

- US: 200g zucchini (spiralized), 50g hummus, 50g cherry tomatoes (halved), 2 large wraps
- UK: 200g zucchini (spiralized), 50g hummus, 50g cherry tomatoes (halved), 2 large wraps

Instructions:

1. Spread hummus on each wrap.
2. Add spiralized zucchini and cherry tomatoes.
3. Roll tightly and slice to serve.
4. Enjoy a fresh and light snack!

Nutritional Info: Calories: 250 | Fat: 10g | Carbs: 30g | Protein: 6g

8. Mango and Black Bean Wrap

Prep: 10 mins | Cook: 0 mins | Serves: 2

Ingredients:

- US: 200g canned black beans (drained), 1 ripe mango (diced), 50g cilantro, 2 large wraps
- UK: 200g canned black beans (drained), 1 ripe mango (diced), 50g cilantro, 2 large wraps

Instructions:

1. In a bowl, mix black beans, diced mango, and cilantro.
2. Spread the mixture onto each wrap.
3. Roll tightly and slice in half.
4. A vibrant and nutritious snack awaits!

Nutritional Info: Calories: 300 | Fat: 5g | Carbs: 60g | Protein: 12g

9. Cabbage and Rice Wrap

Prep: 10 mins | Cook: 20 mins | Serves: 2

Ingredients:

- US: 200g cooked rice, 100g cabbage (shredded), 30ml soy sauce, 2 large wraps
- UK: 200g cooked rice, 100g cabbage (shredded), 30ml soy sauce, 2 large wraps

Instructions:

1. In a bowl, mix cooked rice, shredded cabbage, and soy sauce.
2. Spread the mixture on each wrap.
3. Roll tightly and slice to serve.
4. A simple and satisfying wrap!

Nutritional Info: Calories: 350 | Fat: 5g | Carbs: 70g | Protein: 10g

10. Lemon-Dill Quinoa Wrap

Prep: 10 mins | Cook: 15 mins | Serves: 2

Ingredients:

- US: 150g cooked quinoa, 50g lemon juice, 50g fresh dill, 2 large wraps
- UK: 150g cooked quinoa, 50g lemon juice, 50g fresh dill, 2 large wraps

Instructions:

1. In a bowl, combine cooked quinoa, lemon juice, and fresh dill.
2. Spread the mixture onto each wrap.
3. Roll tightly and slice to serve.
4. Enjoy this refreshing and zesty wrap!

Nutritional Info: Calories: 300 | Fat: 8g | Carbs: 50g | Protein: 10g

CHAPTER 7: GLUTEN-FREE WRAPS

1. Cauliflower Wrap with Grilled Chicken

Prep: 10 mins | Cook: 15 mins | Serves: 2

Ingredients:

- US: 200g cauliflower (riced), 150g grilled chicken (sliced), 2 eggs, 30g cheese (grated), salt, pepper
- UK: 200g cauliflower (riced), 150g grilled chicken (sliced), 2 eggs, 30g cheese (grated), salt, pepper

Instructions:

1. In a bowl, mix riced cauliflower, eggs, cheese, salt, and pepper.
2. Heat a non-stick pan over medium heat and pour in the mixture, shaping it into two wraps.
3. Cook for 5-7 minutes on each side until golden.
4. Fill each wrap with grilled chicken and serve warm.

Calories: 450 | Fat: 22g | Carbs: 20g | Protein: 40g

2. Rice Paper Veggie Wrap

Prep: 15 mins | Cook: 0 mins | Serves: 2

Ingredients:

- US: 4 rice paper wrappers, 100g cucumber (julienned), 100g carrots (julienned), 50g bell pepper (sliced), fresh herbs (mint, cilantro), 30ml hoisin sauce
- UK: 4 rice paper wrappers, 100g cucumber (julienned), 100g carrots (julienned), 50g bell pepper (sliced), fresh herbs (mint, coriander), 30ml hoisin sauce

Instructions:

1. Soak rice paper wrappers in warm water for 10-15 seconds until soft.
2. Lay wrappers flat and fill with cucumber, carrots, bell pepper, and herbs.
3. Roll tightly and serve with hoisin sauce for dipping.

Calories: 250 | Fat: 5g | Carbs: 45g | Protein: 5g

3. Lettuce Wrap with Ground Turkey

Prep: 10 mins | Cook: 10 mins | Serves: 2

Ingredients:

- US: 250g ground turkey, 1 tablespoon soy sauce, 1 teaspoon ginger (grated), 8 large lettuce leaves, 50g shredded carrots
- UK: 250g ground turkey, 1 tablespoon soy sauce, 1 teaspoon ginger (grated), 8 large lettuce leaves, 50g shredded carrots

Instructions:

1. In a pan, cook ground turkey with soy sauce and ginger until browned.
2. Spoon turkey mixture into lettuce leaves, top with shredded carrots, and wrap.

Calories: 300 | Fat: 15g | Carbs: 10g | Protein: 30g

4. Chickpea Flour Wrap with Spinach

Prep: 5 mins | Cook: 10 mins | Serves: 2

Ingredients:

- US: 100g chickpea flour, 250ml water, 100g spinach, 15ml olive oil, salt, pepper
- UK: 100g chickpea flour, 250ml water, 100g spinach, 15ml olive oil, salt, pepper

Instructions:

1. In a bowl, mix chickpea flour with water, salt, and pepper to form a batter.
2. Heat olive oil in a non-stick pan, pour in batter, and cook for 5 minutes.
3. Add spinach, fold, and cook for another 5 minutes.

Calories: 400 | Fat: 15g | Carbs: 50g | Protein: 20g

5. Polenta and Roasted Vegetable Wrap

Prep: 10 mins | Cook: 30 mins | Serves: 2

Ingredients:

- US: 200g polenta (cooked), 150g mixed vegetables (zucchini, bell peppers, eggplant), 15ml olive oil, salt, pepper

- UK: 200g polenta (cooked), 150g mixed vegetables (zucchini, bell peppers, eggplant), 15ml olive oil, salt, pepper

Instructions:

1. Preheat oven to 200°C. Toss vegetables with olive oil, salt, and pepper, and roast for 20 minutes.
2. Spread cooked polenta onto tortillas, add roasted vegetables, and roll up.

Calories: 500 | Fat: 20g | Carbs: 70g | Protein: 15g

6. Quinoa and Avocado Wrap

Prep: 10 mins | Cook: 10 mins | Serves: 2

Ingredients:

- US: 150g cooked quinoa, 1 avocado (sliced), 2 whole lettuce leaves, 30ml lime juice, salt, pepper
- UK: 150g cooked quinoa, 1 avocado (sliced), 2 whole lettuce leaves, 30ml lime juice, salt, pepper

Instructions:

1. In a bowl, mix cooked quinoa with lime juice, salt, and pepper.
2. Place quinoa mixture and avocado slices on lettuce leaves.
3. Roll up tightly and serve.

Calories: 350 | Fat: 20g | Carbs: 30g | Protein: 10g

7. Sweet Potato and Black Bean Lettuce Wrap

Prep: 10 mins | Cook: 20 mins | Serves: 2

Ingredients:

- US: 200g sweet potato (cubed), 200g canned black beans (drained), 8 large lettuce leaves, 15ml olive oil, cumin, salt
- UK: 200g sweet potato (cubed), 200g canned black beans (drained), 8 large lettuce leaves, 15ml olive oil, cumin, salt

Instructions:

1. Boil sweet potatoes until tender, then mash with cumin and salt.
2. Fill lettuce leaves with mashed sweet potato and black beans, and wrap up.

Calories: 400 | Fat: 10g | Carbs: 65g | Protein: 15g

8. Eggplant Parmesan Wrap

Prep: 10 mins | Cook: 20 mins | Serves: 2

Ingredients:

- US: 1 large eggplant (sliced), 100g marinara sauce, 50g mozzarella cheese (grated), 2 gluten-free wraps
- UK: 1 large eggplant (sliced), 100g marinara sauce, 50g mozzarella cheese (grated), 2 gluten-free wraps

Instructions:

1. Preheat oven to 200°C. Layer eggplant slices on a baking tray, top with marinara sauce and cheese.
2. Bake for 15-20 minutes until eggplant is tender.
3. Spoon mixture onto wraps and roll up.

Calories: 450 | Fat: 25g | Carbs: 35g | Protein: 20g

9. Grilled Fish and Mango Wrap

Prep: 10 mins | Cook: 10 mins | Serves: 2

Ingredients:

- US: 200g grilled white fish (like cod), 100g mango (sliced), 2 gluten-free wraps, fresh cilantro, 30ml lime juice
- UK: 200g grilled white fish (like cod), 100g mango (sliced), 2 gluten-free wraps, fresh coriander, 30ml lime juice

Instructions:

1. Place grilled fish and mango slices on wraps.
2. Drizzle with lime juice and top with fresh cilantro.
3. Roll up and serve.

Calories: 400 | Fat: 10g | Carbs: 30g | Protein: 35g

10. Savory Oat Wrap

Prep: 10 mins | Cook: 10 mins | Serves: 2

Ingredients:

- US: 100g oats, 250ml water, 1 tablespoon nutritional yeast, salt, pepper, 2 gluten-free wraps, vegetables of choice
- UK: 100g oats, 250ml water, 1 tablespoon nutritional yeast, salt, pepper, 2 gluten-free wraps, vegetables of choice

Instructions:

1. Cook oats in water until thickened, then stir in nutritional yeast, salt, and pepper.
2. Spread the oat mixture onto wraps and top with vegetables.
3. Roll up and serve.

Calories: 300 | Fat: 8g | Carbs: 45g | Protein: 10g

CHAPTER 8: INTERNATIONAL WRAPS

1. Greek Souvlaki Wrap

Prep: 15 mins | Cook: 10 mins | Serves: 2

Ingredients:

- US: 200g chicken or pork (cubed), 50g tzatziki, 100g mixed salad (cucumber, tomato, onion), 2 large pita wraps
- UK: 200g chicken or pork (cubed), 50g tzatziki, 100g mixed salad (cucumber, tomato, onion), 2 large pita wraps

Instructions:

1. Grill or pan-fry the cubed meat until cooked through (about 10 minutes).
2. Spread tzatziki over each pita wrap.
3. Layer the cooked meat and mixed salad on top.
4. Roll tightly and slice to serve.

Nutritional Info: Calories: 450 | Fat: 20g | Carbs: 40g | Protein: 30g

2. Vietnamese Banh Mi Wrap

Prep: 10 mins | Cook: 10 mins | Serves: 2

Ingredients:

- US: 200g grilled pork or tofu, 50g pickled carrots and daikon, 30g cilantro, 2 large baguette wraps
- UK: 200g grilled pork or tofu, 50g pickled carrots and daikon, 30g cilantro, 2 large baguette wraps

Instructions:

1. Grill the pork or tofu until cooked (about 10 minutes).
2. Spread the grilled meat on each baguette wrap.
3. Top with pickled vegetables and cilantro.
4. Roll tightly and enjoy this vibrant wrap!

Nutritional Info: Calories: 400 | Fat: 15g | Carbs: 50g | Protein: 25g

3. Mexican Burrito Wrap

Prep: 10 mins | Cook: 15 mins | Serves: 2

Ingredients:

- US: 200g cooked rice, 100g black beans, 50g salsa, 50g cheese, 2 large flour tortillas
- UK: 200g cooked rice, 100g black beans, 50g salsa, 50g cheese, 2 large flour tortillas

Instructions:

1. In a bowl, mix cooked rice, black beans, salsa, and cheese.
2. Spread the mixture onto each tortilla.
3. Roll tightly, folding in the ends.
4. Slice in half and enjoy your hearty burrito!

Nutritional Info: Calories: 600 | Fat: 20g | Carbs: 80g | Protein: 25g

4. Indian Paneer Tikka Wrap

Prep: 15 mins | Cook: 15 mins | Serves: 2

Ingredients:

- US: 200g paneer (cubed), 50g tikka masala sauce, 100g mixed salad, 2 large naan wraps
- UK: 200g paneer (cubed), 50g tikka masala sauce, 100g mixed salad, 2 large naan wraps

Instructions:

1. Marinate paneer in tikka masala sauce for 10 minutes.
2. Grill or pan-fry until golden (about 15 minutes).
3. Lay the cooked paneer and mixed salad on each naan.
4. Roll tightly and slice to serve.

Nutritional Info: Calories: 500 | Fat: 30g | Carbs: 40g | Protein: 25g

5. Japanese Sushi Wrap

Prep: 15 mins | Cook: 0 mins | Serves: 2

Ingredients:

- US: 200g sushi rice (cooked), 100g sliced cucumber, 100g avocado, 2 large seaweed sheets
- UK: 200g sushi rice (cooked), 100g sliced cucumber, 100g avocado, 2 large seaweed sheets

Instructions:

1. Spread cooked sushi rice evenly on each seaweed sheet.
2. Layer cucumber and avocado slices.
3. Roll tightly and slice into bite-sized pieces.
4. Serve with soy sauce for dipping!

Nutritional Info: Calories: 300 | Fat: 10g | Carbs: 45g | Protein: 8g

6. Korean BBQ Beef Wrap

Prep: 15 mins | Cook: 10 mins | Serves: 2

Ingredients:

- US: 200g beef (sliced), 50g Korean BBQ sauce, 100g lettuce, 2 large wraps
- UK: 200g beef (sliced), 50g Korean BBQ sauce, 100g lettuce, 2 large wraps

Instructions:

1. Cook sliced beef in a pan with BBQ sauce until browned (about 10 minutes).
2. Lay the cooked beef on each wrap.
3. Top with lettuce.
4. Roll tightly and slice to serve.

Nutritional Info: Calories: 500 | Fat: 25g | Carbs: 40g | Protein: 35g

7. Italian Panini Wrap

Prep: 10 mins | Cook: 5 mins | Serves: 2

Ingredients:

- US: 100g salami, 100g mozzarella cheese, 50g pesto, 2 large ciabatta wraps
- UK: 100g salami, 100g mozzarella cheese, 50g pesto, 2 large ciabatta wraps

Instructions:

1. Spread pesto on each ciabatta wrap.
2. Layer salami and mozzarella on top.
3. Grill in a panini press or skillet until cheese melts (about 5 minutes).
4. Slice and enjoy!

Nutritional Info: Calories: 600 | Fat: 40g | Carbs: 40g | Protein: 25g

8. Thai Spring Roll Wrap

Prep: 15 mins | Cook: 0 mins | Serves: 2

Ingredients:

- US: 100g cooked vermicelli noodles, 100g mixed veggies (carrot, bell pepper, cucumber), 30ml peanut sauce, 2 large rice paper wraps
- UK: 100g cooked vermicelli noodles, 100g mixed veggies (carrot, bell pepper, cucumber), 30ml peanut sauce, 2 large rice paper wraps

Instructions:

1. Soak rice paper wraps in warm water until pliable.
2. Layer noodles and mixed veggies on each wrap.
3. Drizzle with peanut sauce.
4. Roll tightly and serve fresh.

Nutritional Info: Calories: 300 | Fat: 10g | Carbs: 45g | Protein: 8g

9. Lebanese Shawarma Wrap

Prep: 15 mins | Cook: 15 mins | Serves: 2

Ingredients:

- US: 200g chicken or beef (sliced), 50g garlic sauce, 100g pickled vegetables, 2 large flatbreads
- UK: 200g chicken or beef (sliced), 50g garlic sauce, 100g pickled vegetables, 2 large flatbreads

Instructions:

1. Cook sliced meat in a pan until browned (about 15 minutes).
2. Spread garlic sauce on each flatbread.
3. Layer cooked meat and pickled vegetables.
4. Roll tightly and enjoy!

Nutritional Info: Calories: 500 | Fat: 25g | Carbs: 40g | Protein: 30g

10. Cuban Sandwich Wrap

Prep: 10 mins | Cook: 5 mins | Serves: 2

Ingredients:

- US: 100g ham, 100g roasted pork, 50g pickles, 50g mustard, 2 large tortillas
- UK: 100g ham, 100g roasted pork, 50g pickles, 50g mustard, 2 large tortillas

Instructions:

1. Layer ham, roasted pork, pickles, and mustard on each tortilla.
2. Grill in a skillet for about 5 minutes until heated through.
3. Roll tightly and slice to serve.

Nutritional Info: Calories: 600 | Fat: 30g | Carbs: 50g | Protein: 40g

CHAPTER 9: KIDS' WRAPS

1. Peanut Butter and Jelly Wrap

Prep: 5 mins | Cook: 0 mins | Serves: 1

Ingredients:

- US: 1 large tortilla, 2 tablespoons peanut butter, 2 tablespoons jelly, sliced banana (optional)
- UK: 1 large tortilla, 2 tablespoons peanut butter, 2 tablespoons jam, sliced banana (optional)

Instructions:

1. Spread peanut butter evenly over the tortilla.
2. Add jelly on top and sprinkle with banana slices if using.
3. Roll up tightly and slice into pinwheels for fun.

Calories: 400 | Fat: 18g | Carbs: 52g | Protein: 10g

2. Turkey and Cheese Roll-Up Wrap

Prep: 5 mins | Cook: 0 mins | Serves: 1

Ingredients:

- US: 1 large tortilla, 100g sliced turkey, 50g cheese (sliced), lettuce leaves
- UK: 1 large tortilla, 100g sliced turkey, 50g cheese (sliced), lettuce leaves

Instructions:

1. Lay turkey slices over the tortilla, followed by cheese and lettuce.
2. Roll tightly from one end to the other.
3. Slice in half or into pinwheels for easy eating.

Calories: 350 | Fat: 15g | Carbs: 30g | Protein: 30g

3. Fruit and Yogurt Wrap

Prep: 5 mins | Cook: 0 mins | Serves: 1

Ingredients:

- US: 1 large tortilla, 100g yogurt, mixed fruit (strawberries, blueberries, bananas)
- UK: 1 large tortilla, 100g yogurt, mixed fruit (strawberries, blueberries, bananas)

Instructions:

1. Spread yogurt evenly over the tortilla.
2. Top with mixed fruit.
3. Roll up tightly and slice to serve.

Calories: 300 | Fat: 5g | Carbs: 55g | Protein: 10g

4. Ham and Cheese Pretzel Wrap

Prep: 5 mins | Cook: 5 mins | Serves: 1

Ingredients:

- US: 1 large pretzel roll, 100g sliced ham, 50g cheese (sliced), mustard (optional)
- UK: 1 large pretzel roll, 100g sliced ham, 50g cheese (sliced), mustard (optional)

Instructions:

1. Slice the pretzel roll open.
2. Layer with ham and cheese, adding mustard if desired.
3. Close the roll and serve as is or warm briefly in the microwave.

Calories: 400 | Fat: 20g | Carbs: 35g | Protein: 25g

5. Mini Pizza Wrap

Prep: 10 mins | Cook: 10 mins | Serves: 1

Ingredients:

US: 1 large tortilla, 100g marinara sauce, 50g mozzarella cheese, pepperoni slices (optional)

UK: 1 large tortilla, 100g marinara sauce, 50g mozzarella cheese, pepperoni slices (optional)

Instructions:

1. Preheat the oven to 200°C.
2. Spread marinara sauce over the tortilla and sprinkle with cheese and pepperoni.
3. Bake for 8-10 minutes until the cheese is melted. Slice into wedges.

Calories: 450 | Fat: 20g | Carbs: 40g | Protein: 25g

6. Nutella and Banana Wrap

Prep: 5 mins | Cook: 0 mins | Serves: 1

Ingredients:

- US: 1 large tortilla, 2 tablespoons Nutella, 1 banana (sliced)
- UK: 1 large tortilla, 2 tablespoons Nutella, 1 banana (sliced)

Instructions:

1. Spread Nutella evenly over the tortilla.
2. Add banana slices on top.
3. Roll up tightly and slice for fun finger food.

Calories: 400 | Fat: 20g | Carbs: 50g | Protein: 6g

7. Chicken Nuggets Wrap

Prep: 5 mins | Cook: 10 mins | Serves: 1

Ingredients:

- US: 3-4 cooked chicken nuggets, 1 large tortilla, lettuce, 30ml ranch dressing
- UK: 3-4 cooked chicken nuggets, 1 large tortilla, lettuce, 30ml ranch dressing

Instructions:

1. Place warm chicken nuggets on the tortilla.
2. Top with lettuce and drizzle with ranch dressing.
3. Roll up tightly and serve.

Calories: 500 | Fat: 25g | Carbs: 40g | Protein: 25g

8. Rainbow Veggie Wrap

Prep: 10 mins | Cook: 0 mins | Serves: 1

Ingredients:

- US: 1 large tortilla, 50g bell peppers (sliced), 50g carrots (julienned), 50g cucumber (sliced), 30ml hummus
- UK: 1 large tortilla, 50g bell peppers (sliced), 50g carrots (julienned), 50g cucumber (sliced), 30ml hummus

Instructions:

1. Spread hummus over the tortilla.
2. Layer bell peppers, carrots, and cucumber.
3. Roll tightly and slice into pinwheels.

Calories: 250 | Fat: 8g | Carbs: 35g | Protein: 7g

9. Mac and Cheese Wrap

Prep: 10 mins | Cook: 5 mins | Serves: 1

Ingredients:

- US: 150g cooked macaroni and cheese, 1 large tortilla
- UK: 150g cooked macaroni and cheese, 1 large tortilla

Instructions:

1. Place warm macaroni and cheese in the centre of the tortilla.
2. Roll up tightly and enjoy.

Calories: 450 | Fat: 20g | Carbs: 50g | Protein: 15g

10. Marshmallow and Chocolate Wrap

Prep: 5 mins | Cook: 0 mins | Serves: 1

Ingredients:

- US: 1 large tortilla, 2 tablespoons chocolate spread, 30g mini marshmallows
- UK: 1 large tortilla, 2 tablespoons chocolate spread, 30g mini marshmallows

Instructions:

1. Spread chocolate spread over the tortilla.
2. Sprinkle mini marshmallows on top.
3. Roll up tightly and slice for a sweet treat.

Calories: 350 | Fat: 15g | Carbs: 50g | Protein: 5g

CHAPTER 10: CREATIVE WRAPS

1. Sushi-Style Wrap with Quinoa

Prep: 15 mins | Cook: 0 mins | Serves: 2

Ingredients:

- US: 200g cooked quinoa, 100g cucumber (sliced), 100g avocado (sliced), 2 large nori sheets
- UK: 200g cooked quinoa, 100g cucumber (sliced), 100g avocado (sliced), 2 large nori sheets

Instructions:

1. Spread cooked quinoa evenly on each nori sheet.
2. Layer cucumber and avocado slices on top.
3. Roll tightly and slice into bite-sized pieces.
4. Serve with soy sauce for dipping!

Nutritional Info: Calories: 300 | Fat: 15g | Carbs: 35g | Protein: 10g

2. Dessert Waffle Wrap

Prep: 10 mins | Cook: 5 mins | Serves: 2

Ingredients:

- US: 2 waffles, 100g cream cheese, 50g fresh berries, 30ml maple syrup
- UK: 2 waffles, 100g cream cheese, 50g fresh berries, 30ml maple syrup

Instructions:

1. Toast the waffles until golden brown.
2. Spread cream cheese over each waffle.
3. Top with fresh berries and drizzle with maple syrup.
4. Roll up and enjoy a sweet treat!

Nutritional Info: Calories: 450 | Fat: 18g | Carbs: 60g | Protein: 8g

3. Pizza-Flavored Wrap

Prep: 10 mins | Cook: 5 mins | Serves: 2

Ingredients:

- US: 100g pepperoni slices, 100g mozzarella cheese, 50g pizza sauce, 2 large wraps
- UK: 100g pepperoni slices, 100g mozzarella cheese, 50g pizza sauce, 2 large wraps

Instructions:

1. Spread pizza sauce evenly on each wrap.
2. Layer pepperoni and mozzarella cheese on top.
3. Grill in a pan until cheese melts (about 5 minutes).
4. Roll tightly and slice to serve.

Nutritional Info: Calories: 550 | Fat: 35g | Carbs: 40g | Protein: 25g

4. Nacho Wrap with Cheese and Salsa

Prep: 10 mins | Cook: 5 mins | Serves: 2

Ingredients:

- US: 100g tortilla chips, 100g cheese (grated), 50g salsa, 2 large wraps
- UK: 100g tortilla chips, 100g cheese (grated), 50g salsa, 2 large wraps

Instructions:

1. Crush tortilla chips slightly and spread them on each wrap.
2. Sprinkle grated cheese over the chips and add salsa.
3. Roll tightly and grill in a pan until heated through (about 5 minutes).
4. Slice and enjoy your cheesy nacho wrap!

Nutritional Info: Calories: 600 | Fat: 35g | Carbs: 50g | Protein: 15g

5. S'mores Wrap

Prep: 5 mins | Cook: 5 mins | Serves: 2

Ingredients:

- US: 100g chocolate (broken into pieces), 100g marshmallows, 50g graham cracker crumbs, 2 large wraps
- UK: 100g chocolate (broken into pieces), 100g marshmallows, 50g graham cracker crumbs, 2 large wraps

Instructions:

1. Place chocolate pieces and marshmallows on each wrap.
2. Sprinkle graham cracker crumbs on top.
3. Roll tightly and grill until marshmallows are melted (about 5 minutes).
4. Slice and enjoy this gooey treat!

Nutritional Info: Calories: 500 | Fat: 20g | Carbs: 70g | Protein: 5g

6. Macaroni and Cheese Wrap

Prep: 10 mins | Cook: 10 mins | Serves: 2

Ingredients:

- US: 200g cooked macaroni, 100g cheese (grated), 30ml milk, 2 large wraps
- UK: 200g cooked macaroni, 100g cheese (grated), 30ml milk, 2 large wraps

Instructions:

1. In a bowl, mix cooked macaroni, cheese, and milk until creamy.
2. Spread the mixture onto each wrap.
3. Roll tightly and grill until heated through (about 5 minutes).
4. Slice and serve warm!

Nutritional Info: Calories: 600 | Fat: 30g | Carbs: 60g | Protein: 20g

7. Caesar Salad Pizza Wrap

Prep: 10 mins | Cook: 5 mins | Serves: 2

Ingredients:

- US: 100g cooked chicken (sliced), 50g Caesar dressing, 100g romaine lettuce, 50g parmesan cheese, 2 large pizza wraps
- UK: 100g cooked chicken (sliced), 50g Caesar dressing, 100g romaine lettuce, 50g parmesan cheese, 2 large pizza wraps

Instructions:

1. Spread Caesar dressing on each pizza wrap.
2. Layer with sliced chicken, romaine lettuce, and parmesan cheese.
3. Roll tightly and grill until warm (about 5 minutes).
4. Slice and enjoy a delicious fusion!

Nutritional Info: Calories: 500 | Fat: 25g | Carbs: 40g | Protein: 30g

8. Breakfast Smoothie Wrap

Prep: 10 mins | Cook: 0 mins | Serves: 2

Ingredients:

- US: 200g banana (mashed), 100g Greek yogurt, 50g spinach, 2 large wraps
- UK: 200g banana (mashed), 100g Greek yogurt, 50g spinach, 2 large wraps

Instructions:

1. In a bowl, mix mashed banana, Greek yogurt, and spinach until smooth.
2. Spread the smoothie mixture onto each wrap.
3. Roll tightly and serve chilled.
4. A refreshing breakfast on-the-go!

Nutritional Info: Calories: 300 | Fat: 5g | Carbs: 50g | Protein: 15g

9. Spinach and Artichoke Dip Wrap

Prep: 10 mins | Cook: 5 mins | Serves: 2

Ingredients:

- US: 100g spinach and artichoke dip, 100g shredded cheese, 2 large wraps
- UK: 100g spinach and artichoke dip, 100g shredded cheese, 2 large wraps

Instructions:

1. Spread spinach and artichoke dip over each wrap.
2. Sprinkle shredded cheese on top.
3. Roll tightly and grill until cheese is melted (about 5 minutes).
4. Slice and enjoy this creamy delight!

Nutritional Info: Calories: 400 | Fat: 25g | Carbs: 30g | Protein: 15g

10. Chocolate Hazelnut Spread Wrap

Prep: 5 mins | Cook: 0 mins | Serves: 2

Ingredients:

- US: 100g chocolate hazelnut spread, 50g sliced banana, 2 large wraps
- UK: 100g chocolate hazelnut spread, 50g sliced banana, 2 large wraps

Instructions:

1. Spread chocolate hazelnut spread evenly on each wrap.
2. Top with sliced banana.
3. Roll tightly and enjoy a sweet treat!

Nutritional Info: Calories: 500 | Fat: 25g | Carbs: 70g | Protein: 8g

CONCLUSION

As we reach the end of this wrap cookbook journey, I want to take a moment to reflect on everything we've covered and share some final thoughts to inspire your ongoing culinary adventures. Wraps are not only a delicious and convenient meal option, but they also offer a canvas for creativity, nutrition, and cultural exploration.

Recap and Key Takeaways

Throughout this cookbook, we've delved into the fascinating world of wraps, exploring their history, cultural significance, and the many varieties that exist. We learned that wraps can be made with various types of bases—tortillas, lettuce leaves, nori, rice paper, and pita—each offering unique textures and flavours. This versatility is one of the greatest strengths of wraps, allowing you to adapt them to suit your tastes and dietary needs.

We also examined the essential components that make up a great wrap. The key ingredients include proteins, fresh vegetables, and flavourful sauces, all of which come together to create balanced, satisfying meals. By understanding how to select and combine these ingredients, you can craft wraps that not only taste great but also nourish your body.

Summary of Main Learning Points

1. Variety of Wraps: There's a wrap for every occasion, from traditional tortillas to innovative rice paper and lettuce wraps.
2. Nutritional Balance: Wraps can provide a complete meal in one package, balancing proteins, carbohydrates, and healthy fats.
3. Culinary Creativity: The flexibility of wraps allows for endless combinations of fillings, making cooking both fun and exciting.
4. Meal Prep and Convenience: Wraps are ideal for quick meals and can be prepared in advance, fitting seamlessly into busy lifestyles.
5. Cultural Exploration: Through wraps, you can experience flavours and ingredients from around the world, broadening your culinary horizons.

Final Cooking Tips and Best Practices

As you continue to explore the world of wraps, here are some final tips to keep in mind:

1. Freshness is Key: Always use the freshest ingredients you can find. Crisp vegetables and high-quality proteins will elevate your wraps significantly.

2. Don't Overfill: While it might be tempting to load your wrap with as much as possible, remember that a well-balanced wrap is easier to eat and more enjoyable. A good rule of thumb is to fill it about halfway.
3. Experiment with Flavours: Don't hesitate to try new sauces, spices, and fillings. The beauty of wraps lies in their adaptability. You might discover a new favourite combination!
4. Practice Your Rolling Technique: A little practice goes a long way. Rolling your wrap tightly will help keep all the fillings in place. Start from one end and roll it up while tucking in the sides as you go.
5. Use Leftovers: Wraps are a fantastic way to use up leftovers from previous meals. Whether it's roasted vegetables, grilled meats, or even grains, get creative with what you have on hand.

Next Steps

Applying What You've Learned

Now that you've got a solid foundation in wrap-making, I encourage you to put your newfound skills to the test. Host a wrap night with friends or family, where everyone can create their own unique wraps. It's a fun way to bond, share recipes, and discover new flavour combinations.

Consider documenting your wrap-making journey. Keep a cooking journal where you note down your favourite fillings, sauces, and any creative ideas you come up with. This will not only help you refine your skills but also serve as a personal recipe book you can look back on for inspiration.

Advanced Cooking Techniques and Ongoing Education

Once you feel comfortable with the basics, why not challenge yourself with some advanced techniques? Explore making your own tortillas or flatbreads from scratch. This can be a rewarding experience that adds a personal touch to your wraps.

Additionally, look into fermentation techniques to create your own pickles or sauerkraut, which can add a zingy element to your wraps. The world of cooking is vast, and there are always new skills to learn and experiment with.

I also recommend seeking out workshops or classes that focus on global cuisines. Learning from others can provide fresh perspectives and introduce you to new ingredients and methods that can enhance your wrap-making.

Discover More

If you've enjoyed this wrap cookbook, I invite you to check out my other books! Each one offers a unique perspective on various aspects of cooking and meal preparation, from quick weeknight dinners to indulgent desserts. By expanding your culinary library, you'll continue to grow as a cook and discover even more delightful recipes and techniques.

In closing, I hope this cookbook has inspired you to embrace the art of wraps and to see them as more than just a meal. They are an opportunity for creativity, connection, and nourishment. So, roll up your sleeves, gather your ingredients, and dive into the delicious world of wraps. Happy cooking!

Printed in Great Britain
by Amazon